Love to Sew

Christa Rolf

Vintage-Style Gifts for the Home

Search Press

First published in Great Britain 2015

Search Press Limited
Wellwood, North Farm Road,
Tunbridge Wells, Kent TN2 3DR

Original German edition published as
Charmant Shabby Nähen im Shabby Chic

English translation by Burravoe Translation Services

ISBN: 978-1-78221-148-8

Designs: Christa Rolf

Styling: Christa Rolf

Photography: Birgit Völkner & Atelier Lichtwechsel

Step-by-step photography and watercolour drawings: Christa Rolf

Templates: Carsten Bachmann

Repro: Meyle + Müller GmbH & Co. KG, Pforzheim

Printed in China

Place Mat, page 14

Tea Cups, page 16

Cupcake Wall Hanging,
page 24

Button-Heart Pillow,
page 28

Sewing Tins , page 42

Pinboard, page 44

Jewellery Pinboard ,
page 60

Pillow in Stripes, page 62

Love to Sew

Vintage-Style Gifts for the Home

Contents

Introduction

Even as a child I had a passion for old and lovely things. In particular, I collected old fabrics and lace as my family had a long tradition of working with textiles: my great-grandmother was an embroiderer, and my grandmother and mother were both tailors.

My grandmother supported my passion for collecting, giving me old photographs and family documents, and eventually my interest in old-fashioned things led to my passion for the vintage and shabby-chic style.

This book will show you just how charming vintage-style gifts can be. All the designs use fabrics in soft hues with lovely delicate patterns including polka dots, checks and scattered flowers to add variety. Most of these delightful projects are very practical and will come in handy for decorating those old antique pieces of furniture that may have a few knocks or a little flaking paint.

Vintage-style gifts can make a beautiful addition to any home and they take no time at all to make.

I hope they bring you as much joy as they have me.

Christa Rolf

The projects are graded according to how easy they are:

Quick and easy ♡

Requires a little practice ♡ ♡

More challenging ♡ ♡ ♡

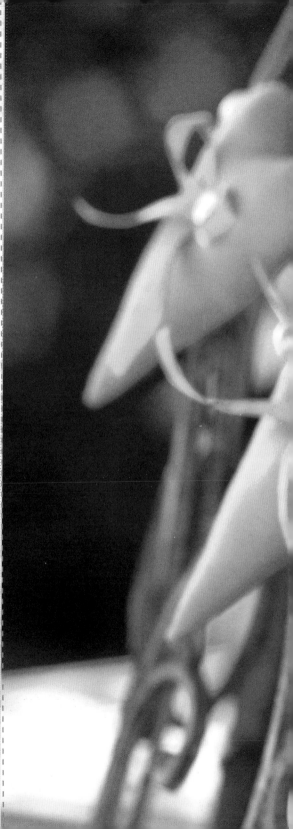

Sewing techniques

Felt appliqué

Felt can be washed, and is perfect for combining with fabric to create decorative motifs. Fusible embroidery fleece with a special coating for ironing can be used as a stabiliser. The adhesive is not very strong, and can be removed without leaving a trace.

How it's done

1 Draw the motifs onto the embroidery fleece, then cut out roughly and iron onto the felt. Cut out both layers precisely to the drawn outline. Pull the top of the embroidery fleece away and attach the felt motifs to the background with a little textile adhesive.

Inserting a zip

A seam allowance of 1cm (½in) is required when sewing in a zip. Most sewing machines have a special foot that makes this job easier (have a look in your sewing machine manual). The zip is usually sewn in using thread in the same colour.

How it's done

1 Zigzag the edges of the fabric cut-outs to neaten them. Draw a line in water-soluble marker 1cm (½in) from, and parallel to, this edge. Fold and tack the seam allowance for the zip to the wrong side along this line.

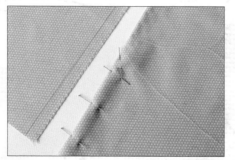

2 Tack the zip under the fabric so that the teeth are very close to the fabric edge, and sew into place using the sewing machine foot.

3 Remove the tacking threads when you have sewn in the zip.

Edging

Edging is used to neaten raw fabric edges. In most cases the fabric edging in this book is made up of long strips of fabric 6.5cm (2½in) in width.

How it's done

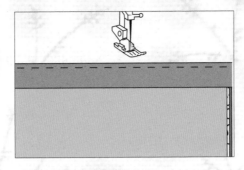
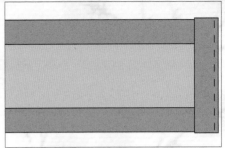

1 Fold the fabric strip in half lengthways, with the wrong sides facing and iron. Open out and fold the two long sides over to the middle crease you have just created and iron again.

2 Unfold your edging strip and place it, right sides facing, against your piece of fabric. The edging strip should be positioned about 0.75cm (⅜in) below the raw edge of your fabric piece. Sew the strip to the right side of your fabric piece, leaving a 5mm (¼in) seam allowance.

3 Fold the edging into position and align the back seam against the back piece of the fabric that you are edging. The back seam of your edging should have the raw edge folded inwards so you can sew the folded edge flush against the back of your piece creating a neat finish and concealing any raw edge.

Bias binding

Bias binding, or bias tape, runs diagonally, or across the grain. Because the fibres of the strip are at an angle to the length of the strip, the fabric is very stretchy and therefore ideal for edging corners and curves. Commercially made bias binding is available in lots of colours and patterns, and has pressed folds, which makes it easier to use, or you can make your own.

How it's done

1 Lay the fabric out flat on a cutting mat. Hold your rotary cutter at 45° to the fabric edge, and cut the fabric with a rotary cutter. Most rotary cutters are marked with the degrees on them. Working from this cut edge, continue cutting the remainder of the strips in the required width. If the length of bias binding required is longer than the length of the fabric, then cut a number of strips of the same width.

2 In order to maintain elasticity, sew the strips together at an angle of 45°. You might find it helpful to draw a line 0.75cm (³⁄₈in) from the edge and sew along this.

3 Iron the seam allowance apart and straighten.

Sewing Frills

Frills are often sewn into the outer edge of a pillow and the frill is included when sewing the seam. To make the frill for a pillow, first measure the circumference of the pillow and multiply it by two.

How it's done

1 Sewn-in frills made from a double layer of fabric can be cut on or across the grain (bias). Cut the strip in the desired width. Fold together with the wrong sides facing, and gather along the raw edge.

2 Loosen the upper thread tension for gathering on your machine, as this will make it easier to pull the lower thread later on (we recommend using tear-proof thread). Set the stitch length to the longest possible (approximately 5), and sew two basted seams close, and parallel to, the outer edge.

3 Gather the frill to the desired length. Pull the two bottom threads to adjust the width. Knot the lower threads to secure the gathering.

Pin the frill to the front of the pillow with the right sides facing. Edge stitch to secure. Place the back of the pillow on top with the right sides facing, sew together and turn the pillow right side out.

Vintage charm for the kitchen

These projects are designed to bring some vintage-style charm to your kicthen. The place mat, bread basket and fabric cupcakes are all made with cheerful patterned fabrics which will complement perfectly those crocheted doilies and quaint old preserving jars you just can't bear to part with.

Materials

- 60cm (23½in) of fabric in a large print pattern
- 60cm (23½in) of fusible volume fleece
- water-soluble marker pen

Cutting out

There is no seam allowance on the pattern piece. To make the template, use a photocopier to enlarge pattern piece 1 as indicated on page 77. Fold a sheet of newspaper into quarters and transfer the pattern piece onto it, then cut it out. When opened up this is the pattern that is used for the shape of the whole place mat.

Tip

The place mat is the shape of a large, vintage-style luggage label. You can also easily make smaller labels in this shape for preserving jars, using pattern piece 11 on page 77.

Place Mat

Size: 45 x 36cm (17¾ x 14¼in)   Pattern piece 1 on page 77

Level of difficulty ♡

Sewing

1 Using the newspaper template, draw the pattern on the back of the patterned fabric with a water-soluble marker pen and cut out with a seam allowance. Take the remaining length of patterned fabric and place the cut fabric piece on top, right sides facing. Place both of these on the volume fleece. Sew all round the three layers, leaving a small opening for turning.

2 Trim the volume fleece back to just before the seam, and the second layer of fabric to the same size as the front. Snip into the seam allowance on the curves and corners to just before the seam to allow for turning. Turn the place mat right side out and sew up the turning opening by hand.

3 Iron to fuse the volume fleece and fabric.

Tea Cups

Size: 7cm (2¾in) high   Pattern pieces 2a and 2b on page 75 and 2c on page 74
Level of difficulty ♡♡

Materials

For one cup and saucer:
- 25cm (9¾in) of blue or pink patterned fabric
- 25cm (9¾in) of white fabric
- 25cm (9¾in) of fusible volume fleece
- knitting dolly
- white wool
- thin wire
- water-soluble marker pen

Cutting out

For one cup and saucer:
The pattern pieces do not include a seam allowance.

Pink or blue patterned fabric:
- 1 piece 20 x 20cm (7¾ x 7¾in) (outside of cup)
- 1 piece 20 x 20cm (7¾ x 7¾in) (saucer)

White fabric
- 1 piece 20 x 20cm (7¾ x 7¾in) (inside of cup)

Volume fleece:
- 2 pieces 20 x 20cm (7¾ x 7¾in)

Sewing

Cup:

1 Iron the volume fleece onto the back of the patterned fabric cut out for the outside of the cup. Transfer pattern piece 2a to the volume fleece using the water-soluble marker pen. Ignore the broken line - this applies to the Cupcake project. Cut out with a seam allowance and sew the short sides together.

2 For the inside of the cup, transfer pattern piece 2a to the white fabric and cut out with a seam allowance, then sew the short sides together.

3 For the bottom of the inside, cut one piece of pattern piece 2b in the white fabric and sew it into the white inside of the cup by hand.

4 Sew the white inside and patterned outside of the cup together along the top edge with the right sides facing. Turn to face the right way then pin the inside to the outside and iron with just a little of the white inside remaining visible along the top edge.

5 For the bottom of the outside, cut two pieces of pattern piece 2b out of the patterned fabric, including a seam allowance. Make a small cut in one of the circles for turning. Sew the two circles together all round with the right sides facing. Snip into the seam allowance to just before the seam, then turn and sew up the turning opening by hand. Sew the bottom of the cup in place by hand.

6 For the handle, knit a 7cm (2¾in) tube using the knitting dolly and the white wool. Bend the wire to the length of the handle, and push into the knitted tube. Secure the ends and pull to the inside. Shape the handle and sew on to the cup.

Saucer:

1 Iron volume fleece onto the back of the patterned fabric cut out for the saucer. Transfer pattern piece 2c to the volume fleece using the water-soluble marker pen, including the darts, and cut out with a seam allowance. Cut out another pattern piece 2c in the patterned fabric.

2 Sew the darts on the two circles of fabric. Sew the two circles together with the right sides facing, leaving a small opening for turning. Turn, and sew up the opening by hand. Draw the broken line in the middle, then sew along it.

Materials

- ♥ fabric scraps
- ♥ thin parcel cord
- ♥ water-soluble marker pen
- ♥ tea
- ♥ small funnel

Cutting out

Fabric:
- ♥ 2 x 4cm (¾ x 1½in) (label)

Cord:
- ♥ 15cm (6in) long

Tea Bags

Size: approximately 4 x 5.5cm (1½ x 2¼in)   Pattern piece 3 on page 74

Level of difficulty ♡

Sewing

1 Fold a fabric scrap in half with the wrong sides facing and transfer pattern piece 3 to the fabric using the water-soluble marker pen, with the dotted line against the fabric fold.

2 Sew up the two outer edges and angled corners in tiny stitches (stitch length 2). Cut out the bag with approximately 2mm (⅛in) seam allowance. Use a funnel to pour the tea in through the open upper edge.

3 Push the cord into the opening and sew up the opening close to the edge, including the cord in the stitches.

4 Fold the cut out fabric for the label in half and push over the other end of the cord. Sew up the three raw edges, working close to the edges, including the cord in the stitches.

Materials

For 1 cupcake:
- ♥ 20cm (7¾in) of blue patterned fabric
- ♥ 20cm (7¾in) of white or pink fabric
- ♥ 20cm (7¾in) of fusible volume fleece
- ♥ synthetic stuffing
- ♥ 1 crocheted flower in white or pink
- ♥ 1 red bead
- ♥ water-soluble marker pen

Cutting out

For 1 cupcake:
The pattern pieces do not include a seam allowance.

Blue patterned fabric:
- ♥ 1 piece 16 x 16cm (6¼ x 6¼in) (base)

Volume fleece:
- ♥ 1 piece 16 x 16cm (6¼ x 6¼in) (base)

White or pink fabric:
- ♥ 1 piece 15 x 30cm (6 x 11¾in) (cream swirl)

Cupcakes

Size: approximately 8cm (3¼in) high   Pattern pieces 2a, 2b, 4 and 4b on page 75
Level of difficulty ♡♡

Sewing

1 To make the base, iron the cut-out volume fleece onto the back of the cut-out blue patterned fabric. Transfer pattern piece 2a (from the broken line to the smaller arch) onto the volume fleece using the water-soluble marker pen. Cut out with a seam allowance and sew the short sides together, right sides facing.

2 For the top of the base, transfer pattern piece 4a onto the back of the blue patterned fabric using the water-soluble marker pen, then cut it out with a seam allowance and sew it into the top of the base, right sides facing.

3 For the bottom of the base, transfer pattern piece 2b onto the blue patterned fabric. Cut out two pieces, including a seam allowance. Make a small cut in one of the circles for turning. Sew the two circles together all round with the right sides facing. Snip into the seam allowance several times to just before the seam and turn. Turn the cupcake right side out and stuff. Sew up the opening in the base and then sew the base in place by hand.

4 To make the cream topping, fold the white or pink cut-out fabric in half with right sides facing and transfer pattern piece 4b using the water-soluble marker pen. The broken line should be on the fabric fold. Sew together along the straight edge. This creates a cone shape.

5 Tack along the raw fabric edge in large stitches. Pull the thread and gather the fabric until the opening is about the same size as the top of the cupcake. Secure the thread and cut. Place the cone on the top of the cupcake and sew on by hand, tucking the raw edges under. Twist the top of the cone to make the shape of the cream swirl. Sew a few stitches through the swirl to secure the shape. Sew on the crochet flower and bead.

Materials

♥ 25cm (9¾in) of striped fabric
♥ 25cm (9¾in) of blue polka dot fabric
♥ 60cm (23½in) of fusible volume fleece
♥ 1 crocheted flower in white
♥ 1 red bead

Cutting out

A seam allowance of 0.75cm (⅜in) is included in the dimensions of the cut-outs and in the pattern piece.

Striped fabric:
♥ 1 piece 70 x 16cm (27½ x 6¼in) (outer)
Blue polka dot fabric:
♥ 1 piece 70 x 16cm (27½ x 6¼in) (lining)
Volume fleece:
♥ 2 pieces 70 x 16cm (27½ x 6¼in)

To make the template for the base, fold a sheet of newspaper in four. Transfer the quarter circle of pattern piece 5 and cut out. This creates the pattern piece for the complete circle of the base. Fold the paper cut-out into four equal segments and mark the folds on the outer edge.

Draw the template circle onto the back of both fabrics, including the marks, and cut out.

Bread Basket

Size: 22cm diameter (8¾in)   Pattern piece 5 on page 76
Level of difficulty ♡

Sewing

1 To make the side of the bread basket, iron a strip of volume fleece onto the back of each of the two cut out fabric strips. With the right sides facing, join and sew each strip into a circle and iron the seam allowance open. Leave about 10cm (4in) of the seam unstitched for turning. Divide these circles into four equally sized sections, and mark each section on one of the long sides.

2 To make the base, take the remaining volume fleece and cut out two circles to fit the shape of the two fabric cut-outs for the base. Iron the fleece onto the back of the fabrics.

3 Pin the two edges to the bottom edges of the side pieces as indicated by the marks. Make sure that the marks are positioned together, one on top of the other. For the outer basket, position the base with the fleece side on the outside and for the inner basket the fleece side of the base should be facing inwards. Sew all round.

4 Pin the two baskets together along the top edge with the right sides facing, and sew all round. Turn the right way out through the opening and sew the opening up by hand. Put the lining into the outer basket and fold the top edge over by about 4cm (1½in). Sew the crochet flower and bead onto the edge.

Cupcake Wall Hanging

Materials

- ♥ fabric scraps in pink and blue patterns
- ♥ 15cm (6in) of fusible volume fleece
- ♥ 10cm (4in) of rickrack
- ♥ 20cm (7¾in) of white satin tape, 3mm (⅛in) wide
- ♥ 1 crocheted flower in white and pink
- ♥ 1 pink bead
- ♥ water-soluble marker pen
- ♥ textile adhesive

Cutting out

There is no seam allowance on the pattern piece.

Pink fabric:
- ♥ 1 piece 11 x 9cm (4¼ x 3½in) (top)

Blue patterned fabric:
- ♥ 1 piece 11 x 6cm (4¼ x 2½in) (base)

Size: 8 x 10cm (3¼ x 4in)   Pattern piece 6 on page 76

Level of difficulty ♡

Sewing

1 Sew the two fabric strips together along one long side (11cm/4¼in).

2 Transfer pattern piece 6 to the back of the joined fabric using the water-soluble marker pen – the dividing line between the top and bottom should be on the seam between the two strips. Cut out with a seam allowance.

3 Place the joined cut-out fabric on a fabric scrap of a similar size with the right sides facing, and place the two on the volume fleece. Sew together all round, leaving a small opening on the bottom edge for turning. Trim the volume fleece back to just before the seam, and the second layer of fabric to the same size as the front. Snip into the seam allowance on the curves and corners to just before the seam. Turn the wall hanging right side out and sew up the turning opening by hand.

4 Transfer the broken lines to the top using the water-soluble marker pen, then sew along them in running stitch. Glue on the rickrack with textile adhesive, and sew on the crocheted flower and bead. Sew on the white satin tape at the top as a hanger.

Designs for the home

Roses were the inspiration behind the patchwork quilt, which is further embellished with crocheted doilies and lace motifs. The matching cushions complete the cosy sitting area and the button heart pattern on the sweet little pillow adds an eye-catching feature.

Materials

- 35cm (13¾in) of beige linen
- 15cm (6in) of striped fabric
- 1 zip, 35cm (13¾in) long
- lots of different buttons in white, pink and grey, 3–20mm (⅛– ¾in) diameter
- water-soluble marker pen

Cutting out

The cut-out sizes include a seam allowance of 0.75cm (³/₈in).

Linen:
- 2 pieces 31 x 41.5cm (12¼ x 16¼in)

Striped fabric:
- 4 pieces 3 x 55.5cm (1 ³/₈ x 21 ⁷/₈in)

Button-Heart Pillow

Size: 30 x 40cm (11¾ x 15¾in), without edging   Pattern piece 7 on page 76

Level of difficulty ♡

Sewing

1 With right sides facing, place a strip of striped fabric on each short end of the linen pieces, for the front and back. Sew along the seam allowance and neaten the seams in zigzag stitch.

2 Transfer pattern piece 7 for the heart to the middle of the front piece of linen using the water-soluble marker pen. Sew on the buttons to fill the heart.

3 Sew the zip in between the front and back (see Sewing techniques, page 8). Sew the front and back pieces together with the right sides facing, leaving the zip slightly open, and neaten the outer edges.

4 Turn the cushion right side out and shape the corners. Stitch along the seam between the linen and striped fabric strips to finish.

Materials

- 45cm (17¾in) in at least nine different cotton fabrics (patterned and plain) in the colour combination cream-beige-dusky pink; you are welcome to use more – we used a total of 14 different fabrics
- 50cm (19¾in) of striped fabric for the edging
- 210cm (82½in) of fabric for the back (150cm/59in wide)
- 210cm (82½in) of fusible volume fleece
- 9 crocheted doilies, 9–14cm (3½-5½in) diameter
- small lace motifs

Cutting out

The cut-out sizes include a seam allowance of 0.75cm (³⁄₈in).

Various cotton fabrics (patterned and plain):
- 88 squares of 19.5 x 19.5cm (7½ x 7½in)

Striped fabric (edging):
- 7 strips of 6 x 99cm (2½ x 39in)

Patchwork Quilt

Size: 144 x 198cm (56¾ x 78in)
Level of difficulty ♡♡

Sewing

1 Lay out the cut-out fabric pieces in eleven rows of eight squares. You can either use a photo for orientation or lay them out as you please. Sew the squares together in rows, and then sew the eleven rows together.

2 Cut out the volume fleece and the fabric for the back, making them a little bigger than the whole front piece. Put the three layers together and secure with safety pins. Quilt in the seam shadow. Trim the fleece and back fabric to the same dimensions as the front.

3 To make the edging, cut one of the striped fabric strips in half crosswise and sew the two cut pieces to another strip making a length of 198cm (78in). This will make one edging strip for the longer side; repeat to make the other long edge. To make the side edges, cut another strip in half from the remaining strips and add one cut piece each to the two remaining strips. Trim any excess and apply these finished strips round the edge of your quilt (see Sewing techniques, page 9).

4 Arrange the crocheted doilies over the quilt and sew on by hand. Sew tiny lace motifs on at the points where the squares meet if you like.

Materials

- 15cm (6in) of pink polka dot fabric
- 15cm (6in) of cream fabric with roses
- 10cm (4in) of cream polka dot fabric
- felt scraps in beige and blackberry
- 35cm (13¾in) of white rickrack
- synthetic stuffing
- 1 reel of extra-strong thread in dusky pink
- textile adhesive

Cutting out

The pattern pieces do not include a seam allowance.

Cake
Transfer the three circular pattern pieces 8a to the back of the respective fabrics, and cut out two circles of each with a seam allowance.

Blackberry felt:
- 1 piece 2 x 20cm (¾ x7¾in) (for the rose)

Beige felt:
- 2 pattern pieces 8b without seam allowance (for the leaves)

Triple Layer Cake

Size: 10cm (4in) diameter   Pattern pieces 8a and 8b on page 78
Level of difficulty ♡

Sewing

1 For each tier of the cake, place the two fabric cut-outs together with the right sides facing, and sew all around in small stitches (stitch length 1.5–2). Trim the seam allowance back to just before the seam. Make a small cut in the middle of one of the fabrics for turning. Turn, then stuff and sew up the opening by hand.

2 Cut a length of extra-strong thread measuring about 200cm (78¾in). Thread a needle and knot the ends so you are using it double. Mark the middle of the back of each tier. From there, push the needle through the cushion to the front. Work once all the way around the outside, returning to the middle of the back and pushing the needle through the front again. Work the needle around the outside a total of six times to make six equally sized segments. Be sure to pull the thread tight every time and secure it on the back. Work all three pieces in the same way.

3 Glue the rickrack around the bottom piece using the textile adhesive and glue the three layers of the cake together.

4 To make the rose, roll the blackberry felt strip up a little bit, working from the narrow end. After 2–3cm (¾-1¼in), turn the strip over and continue rolling loosely, holding the curled shape in position at the base with your fingers. Turn the strip once more and continue rolling until you have rolled the entire strip into the shape of a rose. Sew through the bottom of the rose to keep it in shape. Sew on the two leaves and glue the rose to the top of the cake with a little textile adhesive.

Materials

- 80cm (31½in) of fabric with roses
- 55cm (21¾in) of untreated cotton
- 55cm (21¾in) of fusible volume fleece
- 1 zip, 35cm (13¾in) long
- machine quilting thread in beige
- water-soluble marker pen

Cutting out

To make the pillow template, enlarge pattern piece 9 on a photocopier as indicated. Fold a sheet of newspaper into quarters and transfer the pattern piece onto it, then cut it out. When opened out this will give you the pattern piece for the entire front of the pillow.

The cutting dimensions include a 1cm (½in) seam allowance for the zip; the pattern piece does not include a seam allowance.

Fabric with roses:

- 1 piece 55 x 55cm (21¾ x 21¾in) (pillow front)
- 1 piece 55 x 37cm (21¾ x 14½in) (pillow back)
- 1 piece 55 x 20cm (21¾ x 7¾in) (pillow back)
- For the edging, cut the fabric at an angle of 45 degrees, then cut the remaining strips 3.5cm (1⅜in) wide on the bias. Join the strips to make a length of about 380cm (150in) (see Sewing techniques, page 9).

Patterned Pillow

Size: 40 x 40cm (15¾ x 15¾in) (without edging)   Pattern piece 9 on page 77
Level of difficulty ♡♡♡

Sewing

1 To make your front piece, transfer the pillow template onto your front fabric piece and cut out.

2 To make the quilt lines, use a water-soluble marker pen to draw a diagonal grid pattern on your front pillow piece with the line spacing alternating between 1 and 3cm (½ and 1¼in). Place the front fabric on top of the volume fleece and sew along the grid lines using quilting thread.

3 To attach the zip, take the two pillow back pieces and sew the zip in place along the wrong sides, between the two long edges (see Sewing techniques, page 8). The result should join the two pieces together forming one solid back piece for your pillow.

4 Now place the three layers together (your volume fleece and back fabric piece should be slightly larger than the front piece) and pin together to secure. Trim the back piece and volume fleece so that they are the same size and shape as your front piece. Edge stitch all the layers together neatly.

5 To make the edging, fold your fabric strip in half, lengthways, with the wrong sides facing and iron. Open out and fold the two long sides over to the middle crease you have just created and iron again (see Sewing techniques, page 9).

6 Unfold your edging strip and place it, right sides facing, against your front pillow piece. The edging strip should be positioned about 0.75cm (⅜in) below the rough edge of your pillow front. Sew the strip to the front pillow piece, carefully navigating all the curved edges and leaving a 5mm (¼in) seam allowance. Be sure to hold the strip in a little on the inner corners. You may have to cut the ends of the strip to the required length, and overlap slightly when you sew them on.

7 Fold the edging into position, align the back seam against the back pillow piece and sew to secure.

8 Draw a square measuring 40 x 40cm (15¾ x 15¾in) in the exact centre of the front piece and sew using quilting thread.

A vintage chic sewing room

Surround yourself with delightful little knick-knacks that you can use to create pretty things such as decorated pincushions, enchanting mini-sized tailor's dummies or fabric-covered storage jars,

Materials

- ♥ print patterned fabric
- ♥ old baking tin or cutter
- ♥ synthetic stuffing
- ♥ textile adhesive
- ♥ glue gun
- ♥ decorations such as lace, tiny roses, beads, lace motifs

Cutting out

To make the template, turn a baking tin or cutter upside down on a piece of thin cardboard and draw round the outside. Draw a 5mm (¼in) seam allowance all round. Cut out along the outer contour, and use this as a template for the pincushion. If your baking tin or cutter has wavy sides, use a circle for the template.

Tip

If you are using cutters, you can cover the underside with a piece of firmer cardboard that you have cut out to the right size and shape.

Pincushion

Size: approximately 7–10cm (2¾–4in) diameter

Level of difficulty ♡

Sewing

1 Use the template to draw the shape of the tin or cutter onto the back of the fabric and cut it out, including the seam allowance. Place on a piece of fabric of a similar size with the right sides facing. Sew all around with tiny stitches (stitch length 2).

2 Cut the second layer of fabric to the same size as the top layer. Snip into the seam allowance on the curves several times to just before the seams. Make a small cut in one of the fabrics for turning. Turn, then stuff and sew up the opening.

3 Apply some hot glue from the glue gun into the bottom of the baking tin and push the fabric cushion into the tin. If you are using a cutter, push the cushion into the cutter and secure it from underneath with hot glue.

4 You can decorate the pincushion in a number of ways, perhaps by putting lace around the tin and tying it into a bow, or sticking on lace motifs and roses with textile adhesive. To make the frill between the pincushion and tin, use a darning needle to push the lace into the gap, and secure it in a few places with hot glue. If you are using a tin with wavy sides, you can sew a bead into each groove to decorate the outside.

Materials

- 15cm (6in) of linen
- 30cm (12in) of white rickrack
- 150cm (59in) of white lace, 5cm (2in) wide
- floral lace motifs
- 1 crocheted flower in white
- decorative pins
- 1 pair of angel's wings, approximately 12cm (4¾in)
- 1 wooden stand
- 1 wooden rod, approximately 20cm (7¾in) long
- synthetic stuffing
- textile adhesive

Cutting out

There is no seam allowance on the pattern piece.

Make the template for the dummy from pattern piece 10.

Tip

Instead of the rickrack, you could glue a short length of delicate pompom edging over the top of the lace. The floral lace motifs on the neckline could be replaced by tiny satin roses or narrow lace.

Dressmaker's Dummy

Size: 20cm (7¾in) high (without stand)   Pattern piece 10 on page 79
Level of difficulty ♡

Sewing

1 Use the template to draw the shape onto the back of the linen, and cut out with a seam allowance. Place on a second piece of linen of a similar size with the right sides facing. Sew together all round using tiny stitches (stitch length 2), leaving a small opening on the bottom edge for turning. Trim the second layer of fabric to the same size as the front. Snip into the seam allowance on the curves several times to just before the seams.

2 Turn the dummy right side out and stuff. Push the wooden rod into the stuffing and secure with a little adhesive, then sew up the turning opening, enclosing the rod.

3 Use the textile adhesive to glue the floral lace motifs around the neckline. Fold the white lace into pleats and pin on about 4cm (1½in) from the bottom edge. Sew on by hand and glue the rickrack over the top of the lace. Glue the crocheted flower to the rickrack.

4 Push the wooden rod into the stand and secure with glue. Tie a lace bow around the wooden stand if you like. Glue the decorative pins into the waist to indicate a corsage. Pin the wings to the back.

Materials

For 1 tin:
- 25cm (9¾in) of grey patterned fabric
- 30cm (11¾in) of white lace
- 30cm (11¾in) of cream satin ribbon, 3mm (⅛in) wide
- 100cm (39½in) of parcel string
- 1 crocheted doily, 7cm (2¾in) diameter
- 1 button
- embroidery thread
- textile adhesive
- white paper for label
- metal hole punch
- 1 empty tall tin with a plastic lid (21cm/8¼in high, 23.5cm/9¼in circumference)

Cutting out

The cutting-out dimensions are based on a tall tin. If you are using a different-sized tin, then measure the height and add a 2cm (¾in) seam allowance to the circumference.

Grey patterned fabric:
- 1 piece 21 x 25.5cm (8¼ x 10in)

Tip

For an even more creative vintage-style project, use an old letter case or drawer (a good excuse to trawl around a flea market) and cover it in fabric scraps.

Sewing Tins

Sizes: between 4 and 21cm (1½ and 8¼in) high   Pattern piece 11 on page 77

Level of difficulty ♡

Sewing

1 Wrap the fabric around the tin with the ends overlapping each other. Fold the top of the fabric 1cm (½in) to the inside. Sew the two fabrics together with small stitches where they overlap to fit the tin. Slide into place.

2 Use textile adhesive to glue the white lace to the bottom edge and the satin ribbon to the top. Copy the label (pattern piece 11) onto a piece of white paper and write on it in copperplate or similar pretty handwriting. If you are using tins of different sizes, enlarge the pattern piece accordingly. Cut out the label and glue it on to the tin.

3 Glue the crocheted doily to the lid. Using a metal hole punch, pierce two holes in the lid to line up with the buttonholes. Feed the thread through the holes in the button to the underside of the lid and knot them. Wrap the parcel string around the tin and tie in a bow.

Materials

For the pins:
- ♥ fabric scraps in beige and blue or pale pink
- ♥ 10cm (4in) of fusible volume fleece
- ♥ 10cm (4in) of double-sided fusible adhesive fleece
- ♥ buttons, approximately 1cm (½in) diameter
- ♥ embroidery thread
- ♥ textile adhesive
- ♥ small clothes pegs, 3.5cm (1⅜in) long

For the pin board:
- ♥ wire mesh
- ♥ picture frame
- ♥ stapler
- ♥ white acrylic paint and brush
- ♥ sandpaper

Cutting out

For 1 pin
There is no seam allowance on the pattern piece.
Make the template for the cotton reel from pattern piece 12.

Blue or pale pink fabric:
- ♥ 1 piece 5.5 x 7.5cm (2¼ x 3in)

Adhesive fleece:
- ♥ 1 piece 2.5 x 7.5 cm (1 x 3in)

Pinboard

Size: 4 x 5cm (1½ x 2in)   Pattern piece 12 on page 78
Level of difficulty ♡

Sewing

Pin

1 To make the cotton reel, use the template to draw the shape onto the back of the beige fabric, and cut out with a seam allowance. Place on a piece of fabric of a similar size with the right sides facing, and put both on the volume fleece. Sew all around with tiny stitches (stitch length 2). Trim the volume fleece back to just before the seam, and the second layer of fabric to the same size as the front. Snip into the seam allowance on the curves several times to just before the seams. Make a cut in the top layer of fabric for turning. Turn, then sew up the cotton reel and turning opening by hand.

2 Place the fabric strip of blue or pale pink fabric for the thread with the wrong side up. Fold the two long sides over to the middle and iron. Open out the strip and place the adhesive fleece on it. Iron again to fuse the fleece. Wrap around the cotton reel and secure on the back with a few stitches. Sew on the button with embroidery thread. Glue the peg to the back.

Pin board

1 Staple the wire mesh in the right size to the backing of an old picture frame. Paint the frame, the wire and the backing in white acrylic paint.

2 Once the paint is dry, lightly rub the sandpaper over the edges of the frame. Peg the pins to the wire.

Pink pastel decorations

Create a cheerful atmosphere with hens and hearts!
These soft colours and delicate patterns create a
warm and soothing environment. Combine old and
new tea towels with patterned fabrics, ribbons, tapes,
lace and rickrack.

Materials

- 30cm (11¾in) of pink check fabric
- 10cm (4in) of pink polka dot fabric
- fabric scraps in beige, pale pink and pink
- 2 buttons, 1cm (½in) diameter
- 2 black beads, 3mm (⅛in) diameter
- synthetic stuffing
- wire, 60cm (23½in) long
- rice

Cutting out

The pattern pieces do not include a seam allowance.

Beige fabric:
- 2 pattern pieces 13a (beak)

Pale pink check fabric:
- 2 pattern pieces 13b, one a mirror image (body)
- 1 pattern piece 13c (base)

Pale pink polka dot fabric:
- 4 pattern pieces 13d, two of them mirror images (wings)

Pink fabric:
- 2 pattern pieces 13e, one a mirror image (comb)

Various fabrics:
- 8 pattern pieces 13f, four of them mirror images (tail feathers)
- 2 pattern pieces 13g, one a mirror image (wattle)

Decorative Hen

Size: 25cm (9¾in) high

Pattern pieces 13a and 13b on page 79 and 13c–g on page 80

Level of difficulty ♡♡

Sewing

1 Sew each of the beak pieces into position on the corresponding body pieces. Sew the two body pieces to the base according to the marks (x) on the template. Place the body pieces together and sew all around, leaving a turning opening and an opening for the tail (o); turn. Firmly stuff the head and neck. Put rice in the lower part of the body and fill the rest with synthetic stuffing.

2 To make the tail feathers, put the pieces together in pairs, right sides facing, and sew along the curves. Turn right side out through the opening along the straight edge. Cut the wire into four pieces 15cm (6in) long. Fold the wire pieces in half and push into the tail pieces. Fill with stuffing, but don't make them too firm. Place the four tail pieces over each other, slightly offset, and in line with the opening. Edge stitch together so nothing slips. Fold the seam allowance along the tail opening of the body, to the inside. Place the tail pieces between the fabric layers and sew up the opening by hand, making sure to catch the individual tail pieces in your stitches. Top up the body with stuffing and sew up the turning opening.

3 To make the wings, place two of the pieces together, right sides facing, and sew all round. Snip into one of the fabric layers and turn the wings right side out. Sew all along the outer edge in large running stitches. Stuff with a little stuffing and sew up the turning opening. Sew a button onto each wing and attach the wings to the body by hand stitching them to the sides.

4 Sew together the two pieces for the comb, right sides facing, as far as the turning opening. Turn, and fold the seam allowance around the turning opening to the inside. Stuff, then hand sew onto the head.

5 Sew the two pieces for the wattle together, right sides facing, leaving a short opening for turning. Turn, then stuff and sew up the opening. Fold the crop in half and sew to the neck.

6 Sew on the beads as eyes.

Materials

- 3 pink tea towels, 1 striped, 1 check and 1 floral
- 15cm (6in) of floral patterned pink and white cotton fabrics
- 45cm (17¾in) of white backing fabric
- 45cm (17¾in) of thin fusible volume fleece
- 180cm (71in) of pink rickrack

Cutting out

The cut-out sizes include a seam allowance of 0.75cm (³⁄₈in).

Tea towels:
- 18 squares measuring 11 x 11cm (4¼ x 4¼in) (middle)

Patterned fabrics:
- 2 pieces 6.5 x 58.5cm (2½ x 23in) (border)
- 2 pieces 6.5 x 40cm (2½ x 15¾in) (border)

Table Runner

Size: 38 x 66cm (15 x 26in)
Level of difficulty ♡♡

Sewing

1 To make the front, arrange the prepared fabrics in three rows of six squares. You can either use the diagram below as a reference or you can arrange the pieces as you like. Sew the squares together in rows, and then sew the three rows together. For the edging, first sew the two longer strips for the border to the top and bottom then the two shorter ones to the right and left (see Sewing techniques, page 9).

2 Cut the volume fleece and white backing fabric out, making them a little bigger than the front. Place the front and back together with the right sides facing and pin to the volume fleece. Sew all round, leaving a short opening on one of the long sides for turning. Cut the volume fleece back to just before the seam, and trim the backing fabric to the size of the front.

3 Turn the runner right side out and iron. Quilt along the squares in the shadow of the seam.

4 Sew the rickrack around the middle.

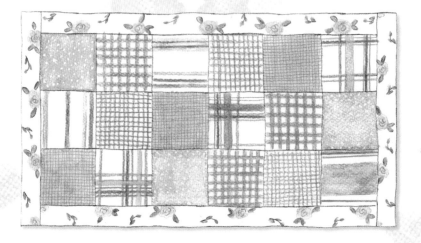

Materials

- 15cm (6in) of beige fabric
- 90cm (35½in) of pale pink ribbon
- 75cm (29½in) of thin white cord
- 5 white buttons, 5mm (¼in) diameter
- 6 white beads, 1cm (½in) diameter
- synthetic stuffing
- embroidery needle

Cutting out

There is no seam allowance on the pattern piece.

Use pattern piece 14 to draw five heart shapes on the back of the beige fabric and cut out.

Chain of Hearts

Size: 30 x 10cm (11¾ x 4in)   Pattern piece 14 on page 79

Level of difficulty ♡

Sewing

1 Place each cut-out heart on a piece of fabric of a similar size with the right sides facing. Sew together all round using tiny stitches (stitch length 1.5), leaving a small section open for turning. Trim the second layer of fabric to the same size as the front. Snip into the seam allowance on the curves several times to just before the seams. Turn the hearts, then stuff and sew up the turning opening by hand.

2 Divide the satin ribbon into five pieces of 18cm (7in) length. Tie into little bows, and sew each one onto the hearts with a button. Using an embroidery needle, thread the hearts and beads onto the cord, alternating between the two. Make a loop at each end of the cord and secure.

Tip

Use a very long embroidery needle or so-called doll needle – used for making Waldorf dolls – to join the hearts together.

Materials

- 3 tea towels, 1 striped, 1 check and 1 floral
- 10cm (4in) of fabric in pale pink and white polka dots
- 15cm (6in) of pale pink fabric in a large check
- 20cm (7¾in) of pale pink fabric in a small check
- 45cm (17¾in) of white backing fabric
- 45cm (17¾in) of rickrack in pink and in white
- 45cm (17¾in) of white lace, approximately 4cm (1½in) wide
- 1 zip, 50cm (19¾in) long

Cutting out

The measurements of the cut-out pieces include a seam allowance of 0.75cm (⅜in).

Tea towel, striped:
- 1 piece 41.5 x 8.5cm (16¼ x 3¼in) (first strip)
- 1 piece 41.5 x 5.5cm (16¼ x 2¼ in) (sixth strip)

Fabric in pale pink and white polka dots:
- 1 piece 41.5 x 7.5cm (16¼ x 3in) (second strip)

Tea towel, check:
- 1 piece 41.5 x 11.5cm (16¼ x 4½in) (third strip)

Fabric in a large pale pink and white check:
- 1 piece 41.5 x 8.5cm (16¼ x 3¼in) (fourth strip)

Tea towel, floral:
- 1 piece 41.5 x 13.5cm (16¼ x 5¼in) (fifth strip)

Fabric in a small pale pink and white check:
- 1 piece 41.5 x 15.5cm (16¼ x 6in) (seventh strip)

White fabric:
- 1 piece 41.5 x 61.5cm (16¼ x 24¼in) (back)

Patterned Pillow

Size: 40 x 60cm (15¾ x 23½in)

Level of difficulty ♡

Sewing

1 Sew the seven fabric strips together, right sides facing, in sequence, and zigzag the seams to neaten. Sew the rickrack and lace on to the front, using the photo for orientation.

2 Sew the zip in between the front and back pieces (see Sewing techniques, page 8). Sew the front and back together with the right sides facing, leaving the zip slightly open, and neaten the outer edges.

3 Turn the pillow right side out and shape the corners.

Tip

There should be enough tea towel fabric left over to sew more pillows in various sizes.

Cake

Size: 22cm (8¾in) diameter   Pattern piece 5 on page 76

Level of difficulty ♡

Materials

- ♥ 1 tea towel, striped
- ♥ 25cm (9¾in) of pink polka dot fabric
- ♥ 60cm (23½in) of fusible volume fleece
- ♥ 70cm (27½in) of wide pink rickrack
- ♥ 70cm (27½in) of narrow white rickrack
- ♥ 50cm (19¾in) of white lace, 4–5 cm (1½–2in) wide
- ♥ 1 pink pompom
- ♥ synthetic stuffing
- ♥ glue gun
- ♥ textile glue

Cutting out

The seam allowance of 0.75cm (⅜in) is included in the dimensions of the cut-outs and in the pattern piece.

Tea towel:
- ♥ 1 piece 70 x 10cm (27½ x 4in) (side strip)

Pink polka dot fabric:
- ♥ 3 pieces 15 x 25cm (6 x 9¾in) (1 for the top and 2 for the base)

Volume fleece:
- ♥ 1 piece 70 x 10cm (27½ x 4in)
- ♥ 3 pieces 15 x 25cm (6 x 9¾in) (1 for the top and 2 for the base)

To make a template for the top and the base, fold a sheet of newspaper in four. Transfer the quarter circle of pattern piece 5 onto the newspaper and cut it out. Fold the paper circle into four equal segments and mark the segment edges on the outer edge. Use the template to draw three circles on the back of the pink polka dot fabric along with the marks, and cut them out.

Sewing

1 Iron the various volume fleece cut-outs onto the backs of the cut-out polka dot and tea towel fabric pieces.

2 Sew the pink rickrack onto the side strip, 3cm (1¼in) from the bottom edge. Sew the strip into a circle with the right sides facing, and iron the seam allowance apart. Fold the ring into four equally sized sections, and mark the four equal fold lines on what will be your top edge. Pin this edge to the fabric circle for the top of the cake – make sure that the marks are lined up correctly and the edges are right sides facing. Sew all round.

3 To make the base, sew the two base circles together with the right sides facing, leaving about 15cm (6in) of the seam open in the middle for turning. Iron the seam allowance apart. Snip into the seam allowance on the curves at approximately 5mm (¼in) intervals to just before the seam. Turn the base the right side out through the opening. Stitch up the opening.

4 Turn the cake right side out and fit the base. Stitch all around leaving an opening for stuffing. Fill with stuffing (not too full), then sew up the opening. The fused volume fleece will provide enough support for the cake to stand up.

5 Use a glue gun to glue the white rickrack around the top edge of the cake. For the cream swirl, roughly tack the lace on one long side. Pull the thread tight to make a rosette, and sew up the bottom with the thread. Glue on the rosette and the pompom to the top of the cake.

Gifts for the bedroom

Give old, white bedlinen a new lease of life – team it up with matching fabrics to create a calming atmosphere in the bedroom. Add embellishments with fabric yo-yos of different sizes.

Materials

- ♥ 50cm (19¾in) of blue check fabric
- ♥ fabric scraps in blue and white
- ♥ 30cm (11¾in) of fusible volume fleece
- ♥ 60cm (23½in) of white lace
- ♥ 1 picture frame, opening 25 x 30cm (9¾ x 11¾in)
- ♥ textile adhesive

Cutting out

Blue check fabric:
- ♥ 1 piece 55 x 60 cm (21¾ x 23½in)

Volume fleece:
- ♥ 2 pieces 30 x 35 cm (11¾ x 13¾in)

Jewellery Pinboard

Size: 35 x 40cm (13¾ x 15¾in)

Level of difficulty ♡

Sewing

1 Remove the back from the picture frame and set aside. Attach the two pieces of volume fleece to each other with a little adhesive, and then stick both to the front side of the picture frame back. Trim flush against the outer edges. Place the cut-out fabric over the volume fleece and position on the long edges of the back. Stretch the fabric tight and secure with long satin stitches. Do the same along the short edges.

2 Cut the lace into two equal-sized pieces. Pin to the fabric and sew on by hand using tiny stitches. Fit the covered back into the picture frame and secure.

3 To make the yo-yos, cut three circles out of the scraps of fabric measuring 5, 7 and 10cm (2, 2¾ and 4in) diameter. Fold the outer edge of the circles approximately 0.5cm (¼in) in to the wrong side of the fabric. With a needle and knotted thread, hand sew along the fabric fold in running stitch. When you are back at the starting point, gently pull the thread to gather the circle. Secure the end of the thread with a back stitch and glue on the yo-yos (see illustration, below).

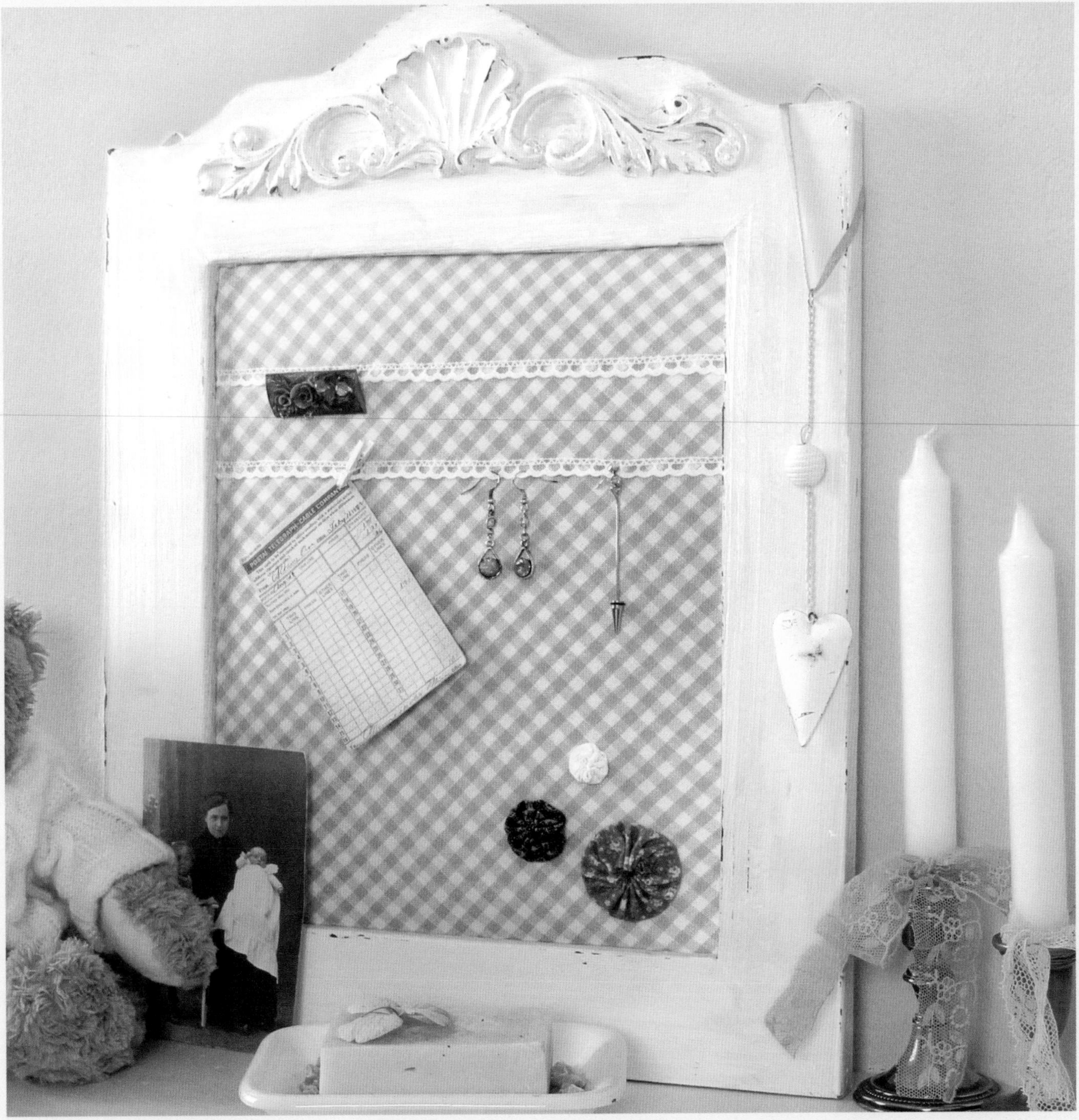
POSTAL TELEGRAPH-CABLE COMPANY

Materials

- 1 old pillow cover in white with crocheted lace
- 15cm (6in) of light blue patterned fabric
- 25cm (9¾in) of blue floral fabric

Cutting out

The cut-out sizes include a seam allowance of 0.75cm (³⁄₈in).

Blue floral fabric:
- 1 piece 20 x 20cm (7¾ x 7¾in), halve diagonally

Light blue patterned fabric:
- 2 pieces 5 x 55cm (2 x 21¾in)
- 1 piece 3.5 x 50cm (1³⁄₈ x 19¾in)

White pillow cover:
- 2 pieces 5.5 x 55cm (2¼ x 21¾in)
- 1 piece 11 x 60cm (4¼ x 23½in) (with crocheted lace trim)
- 1 piece 20 x 20cm (7¾ x 7¾in), halve diagonally
- 2 pieces 6.5 x 40cm (2½ x 15¾in) (edging)
- 2 pieces 6.5 x 36cm (2½ x 14¼in) (edging)
- Back of pillow: cut out the back of the pillow the same size as the finished front. Either use the back of the pillow cover with the finished button placket, or work a back with an envelope closure.

Pillow in Stripes

40 x 30cm (15¾ x 11¾in)

Level of difficulty ♡

Sewing

1 Sew the strips together with the right sides facing (see figure 1) and zigzag over the seams to neaten.

2 Cut out the front on the bias exactly to the required size of 40 x 30cm (15¾ x 11¾in) (see figure 2). Place the back piece on top, with wrong sides facing, and edge stitch to secure.

3 Finish the raw edges with the edging (see Sewing techniques, page 9).

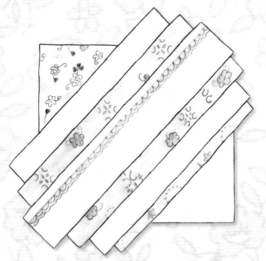

Figure 1

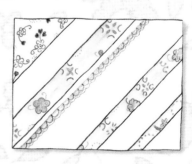

Figure 2

Materials

- ♥ 2 white duvet covers in damask
- ♥ 50cm (19¾in) each of 6 different patterned cotton fabrics in light blue-blue-white
- ♥ 75cm (29½in) of blue check fabric
- ♥ 200cm (78¾in) of extra-wide fusible volume fleece
- ♥ 750cm (296¼in) light blue rickrack

Cutting out

The cut-out sizes include a seam allowance of 0.75cm (⅜in).

White damask:
- ♥ 1 piece 126 x 146cm (49½ x 57½in) (middle)
- ♥ 2 pieces 27 x 151cm (10¾ x 59½in) (edge strip)
- ♥ 2 pieces 27 x 181cm (10¾ x 71½in) (edge strip)

Patterned fabrics:
Cut strips 40cm (15¾in) long and in the following widths out of the patterned fabrics:
- ♥ strips 1 and 2 in 5cm (2in) width
- ♥ strips 6 and 9 in 6cm (2½in) width
- ♥ strips 3, 5 and 8 in 7cm (2¾in) width
- ♥ strip 4 in 18cm (7in) width
- ♥ strip 7 in 15cm (6in) width
- ♥ strip 10 in 14cm (5½in) width

Blue check fabric:
Cut 12 strips of 6.5cm (2½in) width on the bias (see Sewing techniques, page 9–10). Sew three strips together for the edging.

Quilt with Yo-yos

Size: 180 x 200cm (71 x 78¾in)

Level of difficulty ♡ ♡

Sewing

1 Sew the cut-out strips together to make a set (see figure 1). Cut eight sections of 4cm (1½in) width out of this. Sew pairs of these strips together, resulting in a total of four strips of patterned fabrics. Cut the strips exactly to the required length: two to 146cm (57½in) length, and two to 131cm (51¾in) length. Sew the two longer strips to the right and left of the middle piece of the white damask fabric, and the two shorter strips to the top and bottom, forming a square border.

2 Sew the shorter edge strips of the white fabric to the right and left of the patterned strips, and the longer ones to the top and bottom.

3 Cut out the fleece and fabric for the back a little larger than the front. Make the back out of the white bed linen. Put the three layers together and secure with safety pins. Quilt the middle section with diagonal lines and the wide edge with parallel lines. Sew the rickrack parallel to, and round the outside of, the middle section. Finish the raw edges with the blue check fabric edging (see Sewing techniques, page 9).

4 To make the yo-yos, cut 15 circles of 5, 7, 10 and 13cm (2, 2¾, 4 and 5in) diameter out of the blue patterned fabric. Make the yo-yos as described for the Jewellery Pinboard (see page 60) and sew onto the quilt.

Figure 1

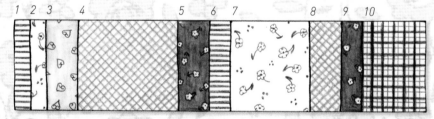

Figure 2

4 cm

Materials

For one heart
- ♥ 15cm (6in) of blue and white patterned fabric
- ♥ fabric scrap in a blue and white pattern
- ♥ 40cm (15¾in) of white lace, 3cm (1¼in) wide
- ♥ 40cm (15¾in) of thin white cord
- ♥ synthetic stuffing

Cutting out

There is no seam allowance on the pattern piece.
Use pattern piece 15 to make the heart template.

Heart & Lace

Size: 10 x 18cm (4 x 7in)   Pattern piece 15 on page 79
Level of difficulty ♡

Sewing

1 Use the template to draw the heart on the back of the blue and white fabric, and cut out with a seam allowance. Place on a piece of fabric of the same size with the right sides facing. Sew together all round the heart shape using tiny stitches (stitch length 2), leaving a small opening for turning. Trim the second layer of fabric to the same size as the front. Snip into the seam allowance on the curves several times to just before the seams. Turn the heart right side out, then stuff and sew up the opening by hand.

2 Wrap the lace around the heart and sew up on the back. Sew a few stitches by hand along the side seams to secure.

3 To make the yo-yo, cut a circle of 7cm (2¾in) diameter out of the fabric scrap. Make the yo-yo as described for the Jewellery Pinboard (see page 60) and sew onto the lace.

4 Shape the cord into a hanging loop and sew on.

Materials

- ♥ 10cm (4in) of blue and white patterned fabric
- ♥ synthetic stuffing
- ♥ scraps of white felt
- ♥ 2 buttons, 1cm (½in) diameter
- ♥ black fabric paint and small brush
- ♥ 15cm (6in) of thin white cord

Cutting out

The pattern pieces do not include a seam allowance.

Use pattern pieces 16a and 16b to make the templates for the bird and the heart.

Bird Hanger

Size: 10 x 7cm (4 x 2¾in)   Pattern pieces 16a and 16b on page 74

Level of difficulty ♡

Sewing

1 To make the bird, use the template to draw the shape onto the back of the fabric, and cut out with a seam allowance. Place on a piece of fabric of the same size with the right sides facing. Sew together all round using tiny stitches (stitch length 1.5), leaving a small opening for turning. Trim the second layer of fabric to the same size as the front. Snip into the seam allowance on the curves several times to just before the seams. Turn the bird right side out, then stuff and sew up the opening by hand.

2 To make the heart, transfer the template twice to the felt and cut out without a seam allowance (see Sewing techniques, page 8). Sew on the two heart wings with the buttons. Paint the eyes and beak on in fabric paint.

3 Shape the cord into a hanging loop and sew on.

Materials

- ♥ 2 old pillow covers in white, 1 with lace and embroidery
- ♥ 10cm (4in) of blue check fabric
- ♥ 15cm (6in) of blue floral fabric

Cutting out

The cut-out sizes include a seam allowance of 0.75cm (³⁄₈ in).

White pillow covers:
- ♥ 1 piece 40 x 40cm (15¾ x 15¾in), cut in half diagonally
- ♥ 1 piece 15 x 50cm (6 x 19¾in) from section with lace
- ♥ 2 pieces 5 x 50cm (2 x 19¾in)
- ♥ 10 x 210cm (4 x 83in) on the bias (frill): cut out several strips of 10cm (4in) width and sew together to the required length

Blue check fabric:
- ♥ 1 piece 5 x 50cm (2 x 19¾in)

Blue floral fabric:
- ♥ 1 piece 12 x 50cm (4¾ x 19¾in)

Back of pillow:
- ♥ cut out the back of the pillow in the same size as the finished front. Either use the back of the pillow cover with the finished button placket, or work a back with an envelope closure.

Frilled Pillow

Size: 35 x 35cm (13¾ x 13¾in) (without frill)

Level of difficulty ♡ ♡

Sewing

1 For the front, sew the white, blue check and floral fabric strips between the diagonally cut lines of the two white triangles, then zigzag the seams to neaten them. Cut into a square measuring 41.5 x 41.5cm (16¼ x 16¼in). Use a glass (approximately 4cm/1½in diameter) to round the corners of the front.

2 To make the frill, fold the strip together with the right sides facing and sew up the short seams. Open out, fold in half with the wrong sides facing, and gather along the long raw edge (see Sewing techniques, page 10). Gather the frill to the length of three sides. Pin to the front of the pillow with the right sides facing. Edge stitch to secure.

3 Place the back of the pillow on top with the right sides facing and sew together. Zigzag the seam to neaten. Turn the pillow right side out and iron.

Materials

For the small birdhouse:
- ♥ 20cm (7¾in) of blue and white patterned fabric
- ♥ 10cm (4in) of blue and white striped fabric
- ♥ fabric scrap in a blue and white check
- ♥ 30cm (11¾in) of white rickrack
- ♥ 60cm (23½in) of white lace, 1cm (½in) wide
- ♥ 10cm (4in) thin fusible volume fleece
- ♥ textile adhesive
- ♥ synthetic stuffing and rice

Cutting out

The cutting dimensions include a seam allowance of 0.75cm (⅜in); the pattern piece does not include a seam allowance.

For the template, copy pattern piece 17a twice and assemble as shown in sketch 17b.

Blue and white striped fabric:
- ♥ 2 pieces 8 x 17cm (3¼ x 6¾in) (roof)

Tip

Enlarge the pattern piece for the large birdhouse (this version will require more fabric). Sew the birdhouse as described for the small one.

Birdhouse

Size: 11 and 16cm (4¼ x 6¼in) high   Pattern piece 17a on page 78
Level of difficulty ♡♡

Sewing

1 Use the template to draw the shape of the house on the back of the patterned fabric and cut out with a seam allowance. With right sides facing, sew up the side seam down the side of the house. To make the bottom, sew up the two opposite diagonal seams. Then sew up the other two diagonal seams.

2 To add the fabric roof, place the two striped fabric pieces together with the right sides facing, and pin both to a piece of volume fleece. Sew all round, leaving a small opening for turning. Trim the volume fleece back to just before the seam, then turn and sew up the turning opening. Sew on the lace on all sides.

3 To make the roof, sew one long edge of the roof to one of the gables. Turn the house the right way out, and pour a little rice in through the unfinished seam. This will give the house the stability it needs. Stuff the rest of the house with synthetic stuffing and sew up the turning opening.

4 To make the yo-yo, cut a circle of 7cm (2¾in) diameter out of the fabric scrap. Make a yo-yo as described for the Jewellery Pinboard (see page 60) and glue it to the house. Glue the rickrack around the house.

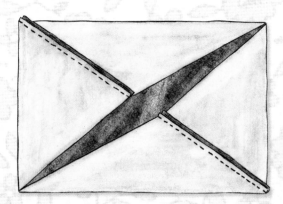

Templates

3

2c

16a

16b

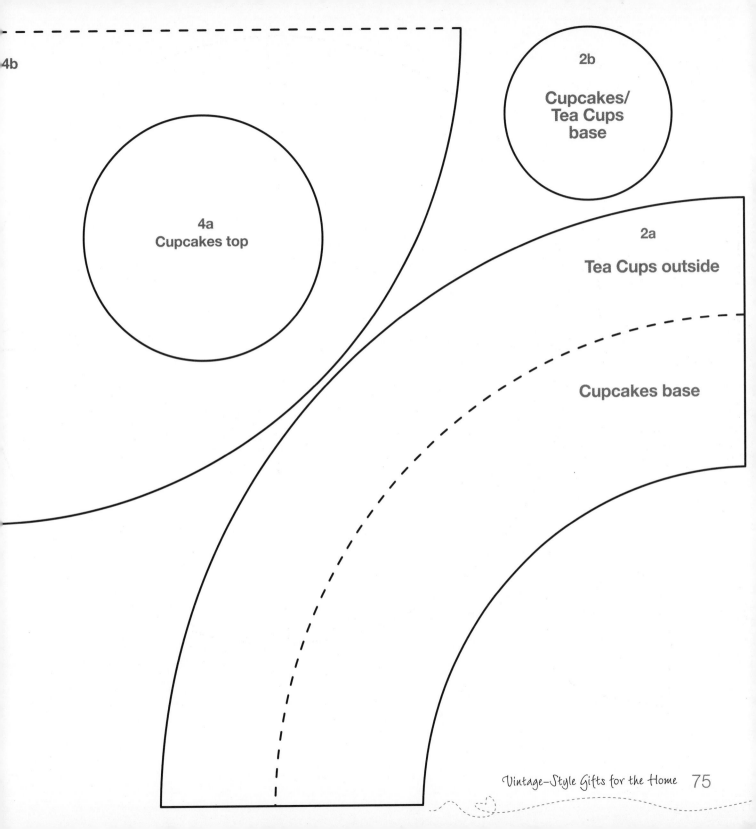

4b

2b

Cupcakes/
Tea Cups
base

4a
Cupcakes top

2a

Tea Cups outside

Cupcakes base

7

5

6

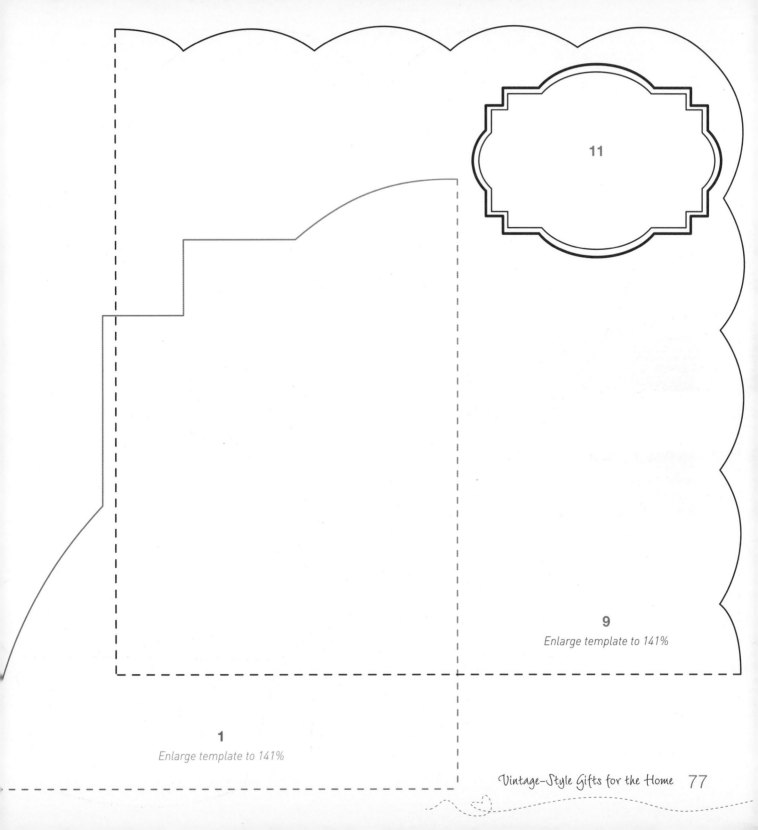

11

9
Enlarge template to 141%

1
Enlarge template to 141%

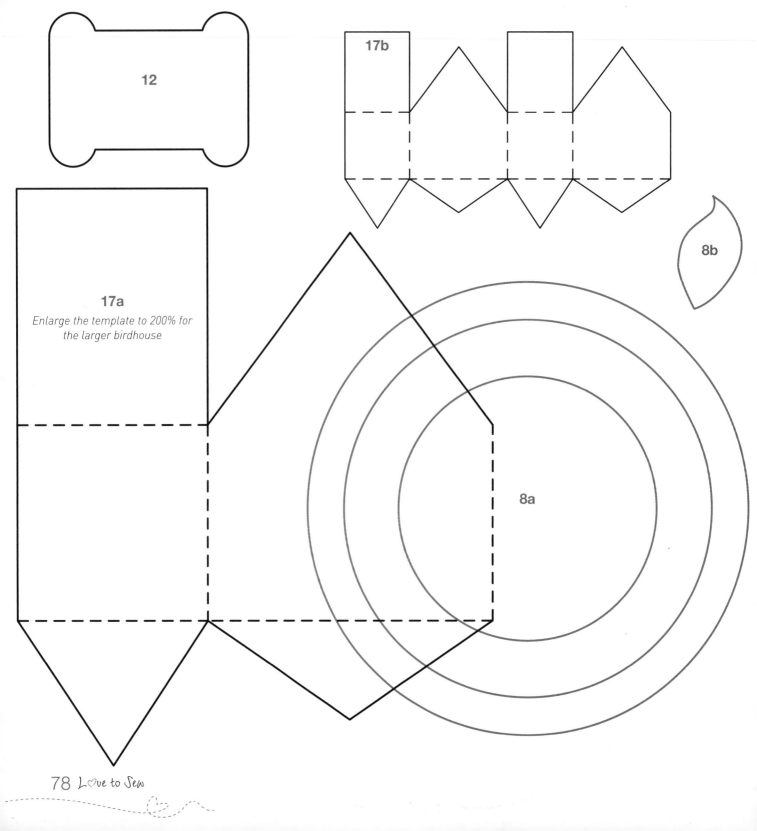

12

17b

17a

Enlarge the template to 200% for
the larger birdhouse

8b

8a

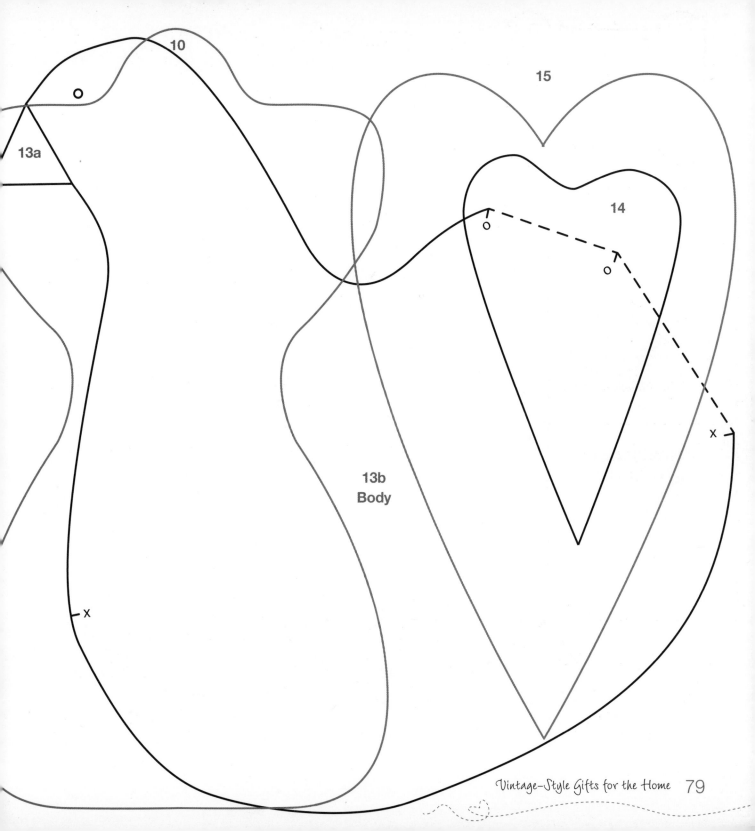

10

15

13a

14

13b
Body

x

x

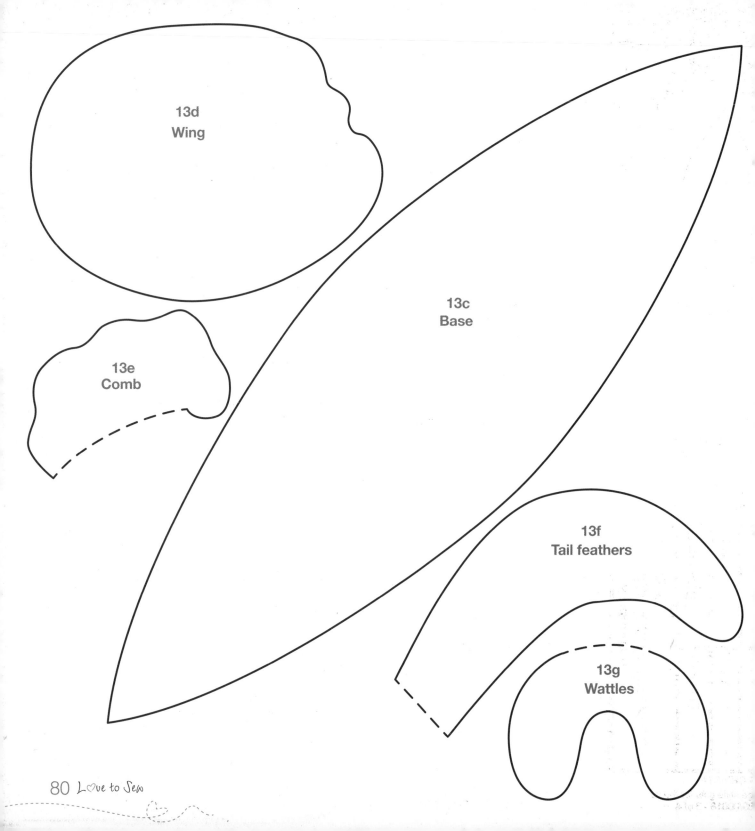

13d
Wing

13c
Base

13e
Comb

13f
Tail feathers

13g
Wattles